Editor
Eric Migliaccio

Managing Editor
Ina Massler Levin, M.A.

Editor-in-Chief
Sharon Coan, M.S. Ed.

Cover Artist
Barb Lorseyedi

Art Manager
Kevin Barnes

Art Director
CJay Froshay

Imaging
Richard E. Easley

Product Manager
Phil Garcia

Publishers
Rachelle Cracchiolo, M.S. Ed.
Mary Dupuy Smith, M.S. Ed.

Author

Janelle Condra, M.A. Ed.

Teacher Created Materials, Inc.
6421 Industry Way
Westminster, CA 92683

www.teachercreated.com

ISBN-0-7439-3221-8

©2004 Teacher Created Materials, Inc.
Made in U.S.A.

Table of Contents

Table of
Contents

(cont.)

Introduction

About This Book

Purpose

The purpose of the *Daily Editing Practice* program is to introduce, review, and practice basic language concepts needed to develop proficient writing skills. This consistent and frequent guided practice promotes skill mastery that will carry over to other writing assignments.

This resource is designed as a ready-to-use daily language program. It can be used in the form of a consumable workbook or as individual reproducible worksheets. It is meant to be used in a guided group lesson and consists mainly of sentences written incorrectly followed by blank lines provided for the students to rewrite the corrected sentence.

Included at the beginning of units 1-6 is a list of language rules explaining each new skill that will be presented. There are nine units, with 20 sentences per unit. Each unit provides daily practice for four weeks. Sentences become longer and skills more complex throughout the book. Assessment pages are included after each unit to check progress. In addition, all skills introduced in a unit are periodically reviewed throughout the following units to reinforce and master skills taught. A cumulative assessment of all skills presented in the book is also included. An overview of skills taught and reinforced is provided on the Scope & Sequence Skills Chart (page 6).

Pages with blank writing lines are included for teachers to write their own sentences. This may be done for additional practice with specific skills or to individualize sentences. The answer keys provided can be torn out if the book is being used as a consumable workbook.

Skill Rules

At the beginning of units 1–6, any new skill presented is included on a "Rules to Know" page. Using these rules as guides, short lessons can be provided as needed by the teacher when introducing a new skill. These rules are not meant to be taught all at once, but individually as they come up in the unit sentences. If the book is not being used as a consumable workbook, these rule pages can be copied and given to students as skills are introduced. Students can keep these pages together in a folder or booklet as their own individual language skills rule book, to be reviewed or referred to as needed. A cover idea for a booklet of this type is provided at the end of the book. In units 7–9, no new skills are presented. These units provide review and practice of previous skills taught.

Standards Alignment

State standards in the language arts/writing area for primary grades emphasize conventions of print and editing written work using correct letter formation, spacing, grammar, punctuation, capitalization, and spelling. This is exactly what the *Daily Editing Practice* program provides. Teachers will be meeting standards requirements, while providing consistent and frequent practice leading to mastery and retention of needed skills for developing writers.

Introduction
(cont.)

Practice Sentences

Most practice pages have two sentences. If the book is not being used as a consumable workbook, sheets can be copied and cut in half. The teacher passes out the sentence sheet for the day to each student and writes the same sentence on the board. The sentence is then read together out loud and the class, as a group, corrects the sentence together. The teacher asks for correction ideas from the students and makes changes to the sentence written on the board as students come up with correct responses. For every correction, the reason for the correction is given as well as how to make the needed change. Conventions of print in writing such as correct letter formation and proper spacing should also be emphasized. Any dates used can be part of the corrections to reflect the current year.

As the teacher corrects each error on the board, the students correct the same errors on their papers. Finally, the students independently rewrite the sentence on the blank lines below. The following is an example of how students make corrections to a sentence during a guided group lesson.

W   I   B   S

will i see beth on saturday?

Assessment

The skill assessment pages are meant to be used at the end of each unit and consist of three of the practice sentences from that unit. On these pages, the teacher reads each sentence to the class and the students independently make corrections to the sentences without recopying them. This gives the teacher a way to assess students progress and determine the need for any additional reinforcement to the class or individual student in specific skill areas. The points possible represent the total number of words, groups of numbers, and punctuation marks in the three sentences and are indicated on the assessment page. Each word, group of numbers, and punctuation mark is awarded one point and is counted as either totally correct or incorrect. This means counting all words, numbers, and punctuation whether incorrectly written or not. For example, if a student capitalizes a word that does not need to be capitalized, it would be counted as wrong, even though it is written correctly in the sentence above. The total number of possible points for each unit assessment is calculated and written at the bottom of each assessment page.

The cumulative assessment includes a sample of all skills presented in the book. Since this assessment is much longer, having students complete it in more than one session is recommended.

Scope & Sequence Skills Chart

• = Skill Introduced
+ = Skill Reinforced

	Units								
	1	2	3	4	5	6	7	8	9
Capitalization									
Beginning of a sentence	•	+	+	+	+	+	+	+	+
The word I	•	+	+	+	+	+	+	+	+
Proper nouns	•	+	+	+	+	+	+	+	+
Days of the week	•	+	+	+	+	+	+	+	+
Months of the year	•	+	+	+	+	+	+	+	+
Name title	•	+	+	+	+	+	+	+	+
Holidays		•	+	+	+	+	+	+	+
Book title			•	+	+	+	+	+	+
Letter greeting/closing			•	+	+	+	+	+	+
First word in a quote				•	+	+	+	+	+
Address					•	+	+	+	+
Punctuation									
Sentence ending period	•	+	+	+	+	+	+	+	+
Sentence ending question mark	•	+	+	+	+	+	+	+	+
Period in an abbreviation	•	+	+	+	+	+	+	+	+
Comma in a date	•	+	+	+	+	+	+	+	+
Apostrophe in a singular possessive	•	+	+	+	+	+	+	+	+
Commas in a series		•	+	+	+	+	+	+	+
Comma between city and state		•	+	+	+	+	+	+	+
Sentence ending exclamation mark		•	+	+	+	+	+	+	+
Underline in a book title			•	+	+	+	+	+	+
Commas in letter greeting/closing			•	+	+	+	+	+	+
Colon/time			•	+	+	+	+	+	+
Apostrophe in a contraction				•	+	+	+	+	+
Quotation marks				•	+	+	+	+	+
Comma in a quotation				•	+	+	+	+	+
Grammar & Usage									
Homophones	•	+	+	+	+	+	+	+	+
Add s to make nouns plural		•	+	+	+	+	+	+	+
Word order		•	+	+	+	+	+	+	+
Pronoun usage		•	+	+	+	+	+	+	+
Add es to make nouns plural			•	+	+	+	+	+	+
Misspelled/misused verbs			•	+	+	+	+	+	+
Verb tenses					•	+	+	+	+
Identify irregular past tense verbs					•	+	+	+	+
Subject/verb agreement					•	+	+	+	+
Irregular plural nouns						•	+	+	+
Double negatives						•	+	+	+
Double subjects						•	+	+	+

Unit 1
Rules to Know

****

1. A *sentence* is a group of words that tells a complete thought. Capitalize the first word in a sentence.

   ➢ **The dog is black.**

2. Capitalize the word *I*.

   ➢ **Tom and I are friends.**

3. *Nouns* are words that name people, places, things, and animals. Proper nouns name specific people, places, things, and animals and begin with a capital letter. Capitalize the names of people or pets.

   ➢ **I will play with Dan.**

   ➢ **My cat is named Puff.**

4. Capitalize the names of specific places.

   ➢ **That is Park School.**

   ➢ **Is this Maple Street?**

   ➢ **Can we eat at Pat's Pizza?**

   ➢ **Do you live in Dallas, Texas?**

5. A *statement* is a sentence that tells something. Put a period at the end of a telling sentence.

   ➢ **My house is white.**

6. A question is a sentence that asks something. Put a question mark at the end of an *asking sentence*.

   ➢ **Do you have a pet?**

7. Capitalize the days of the week and months of the year.

   ➢ **Today is Saturday.**

   ➢ **My birthday is in May.**

****

8. An *abbreviation* is a short form of a word. Capitalize name titles and put a period after ones that have been shortened into an abbreviation.

          Mister — Mr.   Misses — Mrs.   Doctor — Dr.

> **His friend is <u>Mr.</u> Brown.**

> **My teacher is <u>Mrs.</u> Lee.**

> **<u>Dr</u>. Rob is at the hospital.**

> **<u>Miss</u> Smith lives here.**

9. A *homophone* is a word that sounds the same as another word but has a different spelling or meaning. Use the homophones *to, two, too* correctly.

    to — in the direction of   *two* — names a number   *too* — also, or more than enough

> **I went <u>to</u> school.**

> **Did you read <u>two</u> books?**

> **The box was <u>too</u> heavy to lift.**

> **She wants some candy, <u>too</u>.**

10. A comma signals a pause. Use a comma in a date to separate the day and year.

> **She was born on September 10<u>,</u> 2003.**

> **The race was on July 4<u>,</u> 2004.**

11. A possessive noun shows ownership. Use an apostrophe and an *s* ('s) after a noun to show something belongs to one person or thing.

> **That is Beth<u>'s</u> room.**

> **My mom<u>'s</u> name is Pat.**

i see ben

i will go with bob

Name: _____ Date: _____

we can play with jill

Name: _____ Date: _____

do you see belinda

10

megan and i are
friends

can bill get the ball

my teacher is mrs
white

can i go with david

will i see beth on saturday

miss king has a dog named spot

does fall begin in
september or october

my birthday is in
september

toms dad is mr glen smith

do we go two school on sunday

i like two eat at tasty burger

marys family has to dogs

my sister was born on
july 15 2003

is tims birthday in
may or june

jeff and i go two west school

my moms car is red black and gray

Unit 1 — Assessment

Name: _____ Date: _____

1. my teacher is mrs white

2. will i see beth on saturday

3. is tims birthday in may or june

Score all words, group of numbers, or punctuation marks in these sentences as one point each, whether or not a correction is needed.

Score: _____ /23 _____ %

Unit 1 — Assessment

Answer Key

M   M

1. my teacher is mrs.

W

white.

W   I   B

2. will i see beth on

S

saturday?

I T

3. is tim's birthday in

M   J

may or june?

Unit 1
Answer Key

****

1. I see Ben.

2. I will go with Bob.

3. We can play with Jill.

4. Do you see Belinda?

5. Megan and I are friends.

6. Can Bill get the ball?

7. My teacher is Mrs. White.***

8. Can I go with David?

9. Will I see Beth on Saturday?***

10. Miss King has a dog named Spot.

11. Does fall begin in September or October?

12. My birthday is in September.

13. Tom's dad is Mr. Glen Smith.

14. Do we go to school on Sunday?

15. I like to eat at Tasty Burger.

16. Mary's family has two dogs.

17. My sister was born on July 15, 2003.

18. Is Tim's birthday in May or June?***

19. Jeff and I go to West School.

20. My mom's car is red, black, and gray.

***Unit 1 Assessment questions

Unit 2
Rules to Know

1. A *singular noun* names one person, place, thing, or animal. A *plural noun* names more than one person, place, thing, or animal. Add *s* to most nouns to make them plural.

    ➢ **Where are the do<u>g</u>s?**
    ➢ **The car<u>s</u> went fast.**

2. A *comma* signals a pause. A *series* is a list of three or more items. Use a comma to separate three or more words or groups of words in a series.

    ➢ **Is your favorite food pizza, hamburger, or macaroni?**
    ➢ **At the zoo he saw a tiger, an elephant, and a bear.**

3. A *comma* signals a pause. Put a comma between the city and state.

    ➢ **Do you live in Madison, Wisconsin?**

4. Capitalize the names of holidays.

    ➢ **We have fun on <u>H</u>alloween.**
    ➢ **We eat a big meal on <u>T</u>hanksgiving.**

5. A *pronoun* is a word that is used in place of a noun. Use the pronouns *they* and *them* correctly.

    use ***they*** — when a group is doing something

    use ***them*** — when something is happening to a group.

    ➢ **<u>They</u> are going home.**
    ➢ **Will you help <u>them</u>?**

6. A *subject* tells how or what the sentence is about. In a sentence with more than one subject where *I* is used, *I* is written last.

    ➢ ***Tim and I* went to the movie.**

bob and nan got a lot of toy on saturday

do you have one cat or to cat

fall leaves are red

yellow and brown

Name: _____ Date: _____ Unit 2 - 4

does mr wills teach at

oak school

today the date is october 15 2004

is halloween in october november or december

did them go two
school in the fall

the principal at north
school is miss brown

i and brandon like

halloween

---

does jims costume look

scary

is pauls pizza parlor on main street

kim has a cat a dog and a bird

will halloween be on october 31 2004

mrs blacks costume will be a cat

is your favorite color

pink blue or purple

the three boy went

fishing every sunday

are them going on a
trip two canada

my dads house is by
blue river in wisconsin

on halloween i want candy cookies and gum

are you moving two orlando florida

Unit 2 — Assessment

Name: _____   Date: _____

1. *is halloween in october november or december*

2. *are you moving two orlando florida*

3. *the three boy went fishing every sunday*

Score all words, group of numbers, or punctuation marks in these sentences as one point each, whether or not a correction is needed.

Score: _____ /26 _____ %

Unit 2 — Assessment

Answer Key

1. I H O
   is halloween in october,
   N D
   november, or december?

2. A to
   are you moving two
   O F
   orlando, florida?

3. T
   the three boys went
   S
   fishing every sunday.

Unit 2
Answer Key

1. Bob and Nan got a lot of toys on Saturday.

2. Do you have one cat or two cats?

3. Fall leaves are red, yellow, and brown.

4. Does Mr. Wills teach at Oak School?

5. Today the date is October 15, 2004.

6. Is Halloween in October, November, or December?***

7. Did they go to school in the fall?

8. The principal at North School is Miss Brown.

9. Brandon and I like Halloween.

10. Does Jim's costume look scary?

11. Is Paul's Pizza Parlor on Main Street?

12. Kim has a cat, a dog, and a bird.

13. Will Halloween be on October 31, 2004?

14. Mrs. Black's costume will be a cat.

15. Is your favorite color pink, blue, or purple?

16. The three boys went fishing every Sunday.***

17. Are they going on a trip to Canada?

18. My dad's house is by Blue River in Wisconsin.

19. On Halloween I want candy, cookies, and gum.

20. Are you moving to Orlando, Florida?***

*** **Unit 2 Assessment answers**

Unit 3

Rules to Know

1. An *exclamation* is a sentence that expresses strong feelings. It ends with an exclamation mark.

   ➢ **We won the game!**

2. A *homophone* is a word that sounds the same as another word but has a different spelling or meaning. Learn to use homophones correctly. Here are some examples:

red → read	here → hear	for → four
be → bee	know → no	rode → road
sea → see	weak → week	to → two → too
one → won	buy → by	their → there → they're
knight → night	would → wood	

3. When writing the title of a book, underline the entire title and capitalize the first word, the last word, and each important word.

   ➢ **Have you read the book <u>Hansel and Gretel</u>?**

4. A singular noun names one person, place, thing, or animal. A plural noun names more than one person, place, thing, or animal. Add *s* to most nouns to make them plural. Add *es* to words that end in *s*, *ch*, *sh*, *x*, and *z*.

   ➢ **Where are the box<u>es</u>?**
   ➢ **The dish<u>es</u> need to be washed.**
   ➢ **I had to take two bus<u>es</u> to get home.**

5. A subject tells who or what the sentence is about. In a sentence with more than one subject where one of the subjects is *you*, write *yourself* last. Use the word *I* instead of *me* when you are doing the action.

   ➢ **<u>Me and Tim</u> went to the movie.** (incorrect)
   ➢ **<u>Tim and I</u> went to the movie.** (correct)

Unit 3

Rules to Know

6. A *pronoun* is a word that is used in place of a noun. Use the pronouns we/us, she/he, and her/him correctly.

   use **we** — when you and others are doing something

   use **she/he** — when a person is doing something

   use **us** — when something happens to you and others

   use **her/him** — when something happens to a person

   ➢ <u>We</u> went to school.

   ➢ <u>She</u> gave <u>him</u> a ride.

   ➢ <u>They</u> gave the trophy to <u>us</u>.

   ➢ <u>He</u> took <u>her</u> to the movie.

7. Do not spell verbs incorrectly, as they are often mispronounced.

   ➢ We are <u>gonna</u> go now. → We are <u>going to</u> go now.

   ➢ We <u>wanna</u> leave. → We <u>want to</u> leave.

8. A *colon* is used between the hour and minutes when writing the time of day.

   ➢ We went to school at 8<u>:</u>00.

9. A friendly letter has five parts: date, greeting, body, closing, and signature. Capitalize the first word of the greeting in a letter. Put a comma after the greeting in a friendly letter.

   ➢ Dear Bob<u>,</u>   ➢ Hello Jill<u>,</u>

10. Capitalize the first word of the closing in a letter. Put a comma after the closing.

    ➢ Your friend<u>,</u>   ➢ Love always<u>,</u>

11. Indent the first word of the body of a friendly letter by moving the first word a little to the right. Move the closing and signature to the right so that they line up with the date.

    November 5, 2004

    Dear Bob,

    　　How are you? Did you get a new bike on Saturday?

    　　　　　　Your friend,

    　　　　　　Jon

that mans house is on
fire

jack has too cat and
to dog's

will it bee windy rainy

or snowy on monday

where is mr hansons

house

did her read a book called

the tiny pumpkin

me and meg had two

wash the dishs

it was a surprise two

sea them last knight

what holiday is on

november 27 2004

those box were to
heavy for max too lift

is jills favorite book
the three pigs

november 1 2004

dear mary

how is your knew school

we miss you

your friend

jen

the too boy's will bee

hear at 100 on sunday

we are gonna bee late

if we do not hurry

will thanksgiving bee on

wednesday or thursday

him was two short too

reach the shelf

do you wanna go two cleveland ohio

us here the recess bell ring at 1000

november 18 2004

dear grandma

me and stan hope you

can come two visit soon

with love

brad

them red the cat in
the hat by dr seuss

on thanksgiving i like
turkey potatoes and pie

Unit 3 — Assessment

Name: _____ Date: _____

1. did her read a book called the tiny pumpkin

2. those box were to heavy for max too lift

3. us here the recess bell ring at 1000

Score all words, group of numbers, or punctuation marks in these sentences as one point each, whether or not a correction is needed.

Score: _____ /31 _____ %

Unit 3 — Assessment

Answer Key

D   she

1. did her read a book called

T   T   P

the tiny pumpkin?

T   too

2. those boxes were to

        M   to

heavy for max too lift.

We hear

3. us here the recess bell

ring at 10:00.

1. That man's house is on fire!

2. Jack has two cats and two dogs.

3. Will it be windy, rainy, or snowy on Monday?

4. Where is Mr. Hanson's house?

5. Did she read a book called <u>The Tiny Pumpkin</u>?***

6. Meg and I had to wash the dishes.

7. It was a surprise to see them last night!

8. What holiday is on November 27, 2004?

9. Those boxes were too heavy for Max to lift.***

10. Is Jill's favorite book <u>The Three Pigs</u>?

11.   November 1, 2004

    Dear Mary,

        How is your new school? We miss you.

            Your friend,

            Jen

12. The two boys will be here at 1:00 on Sunday.

13. We are going to be late if we do not hurry!

14. Will Thanksgiving be on Wednesday or Thursday?

15. He was too short to reach the shelf.

16. Do you want to go to Cleveland, Ohio?

17. We hear the recess bell ring at 10:00.***

18.   November 18, 2004

    Dear Grandma,

        Stan and I hope you can come to visit soon.

            With love,

            Brad

19. They read <u>The Cat in the Hat</u> by Dr. Seuss.

20. On Thanksgiving I like turkey, potatoes, and pie.

***Unit 3 Assessment answers**

Unit 4

Rules to Know

1. A *contraction* is a word made by joining two words. When joining the words, a letter or letters are left out. An *apostrophe* is put in the word at the spot where the letter or letters are missing.

   ➢ **We are going home. We're going home.**
   ➢ **She did not see him. She didn't see him.**

2. Do not use the slang word *ain't*.

   ➢ **We ain't late.** (incorrect)
   ➢ **We are not late.** (correct)

3. A *quotation* shows the speaker's exact words. Use quotation marks at the beginning and ending of a quotation to show where the speaker started and stopped talking. Begin a quotation with a capital letter.

   ➢ **"Today we are going to the zoo," said Bill.**
   ➢ **Mary asked, "Can we go with you?"**

4. Use the correct punctuation to separate a quotation from the rest of the sentence. In a telling sentence, use a comma between the quotation and the rest of the sentence and end the sentence with a period.

   ➢ **Dad said, "It is raining."**
   ➢ **"It is raining," said Dad.**

5. In an asking sentence, use a question mark at the end of the quotation. If the quotation is before the speaker's name, put a period at the end of the sentence. If the speaker's name is before the quotation, separate the quotation with a comma.

   ➢ **"Where are we going?" asked Jane.**
   ➢ **Jane asked, "Where are we going?"**

6. In an *exclamation,* use an exclamation mark at the end of the quotation. If the quotation is before the speaker's name, put a period at the end of the sentence. If the speaker's name is before the quotation, separate the quotation with a comma.

   ➢ **"That house is on fire!" shouted the man.**
   ➢ **The man shouted, "That house is on fire!"**

my friends birthday was on friday said bill

today ain't december 9 2004

is christmas in

november or december

me and scott cant go

said ron

them red the book the knight before christmas

for christmas i want a book a toy and a pet

what did you do on monday asked katlin

what holiday is on december 25 2004

santa said its very cold at the north pole

we have two go home at 330 said the girl's

december 11 2004

dear santa

ive been good this year

hows rudolph doing

your friend

kate

ain't santas wife

called mrs claus

were going two miami

florida four vacation

will christmas bee on a saturday or sunday

santa said merry christmas everybody

i have two many list's
too read said santa

mrs beck said their is
know school next weak

december 18 2004

dear grandma

im so glad youre

coming for christmas

with love

jake

do you wanna go too the
knew movie said ben

well need six bus for
the trip said dr dennis

Unit 4 — Assessment

Name: _____ Date: _____

1. today ain't december 9 2004

2. what did you do on monday asked katlin

3. santa said its very cold at the north pole

Score all words, group of numbers, or punctuation marks in these sentences as one point each, whether or not a correction is needed.

Score: _____ /34 _____ %

Unit 4 — Assessment

Answer Key

T   isn't

1. ~~today~~ ~~ain't~~

D

   ~~december~~ 9, 2004.

W

2. "~~what~~ did you do on

M   K

   ~~monday~~?" asked ~~katlin~~.

S   I

3. ~~santa~~ said, "~~it's~~ very

        N   P (! or .)

   cold at the ~~north pole~~!"

Unit 4

Answer Key

1. "My friend's birthday was on Friday," said Bill.

2. Today isn't December 9, 2004.***

3. Is Christmas in November or December?

4. "Scott and I can't go," said Ron.

5. They read the book <u>The Night Before Christmas</u>.

6. For Christmas I want a book, a toy, and a pet.

7. "What did you do on Monday?" asked Katlin.***

8. What holiday is on December 25, 2004?

9. Santa said, "It's very cold at the North Pole!"***

10. "We have to go home at 3:30," said the girls.

11.   December 11, 2004
    Dear Santa,
      I've been good this year. How's Rudolph doing?
            Your friend,
            Kate

12. Isn't Santa's wife called Mrs. Claus?

13. We're going to Miami, Florida for vacation.

14. Will Christmas be on a Saturday or Sunday?

15. Santa said, "Merry Christmas everybody!"

16. "I have too many lists to read!" said Santa.

17. Mrs. Beck said, "There is no school next week."

18.   December 18, 2004
    Dear Grandma,
      I'm so glad you're coming for Christmas!
            Love,
            Jake

19. "Do you want to go to the new movie?" said Ben.

20. "We'll need six buses for the trip," said Dr. Dennis.

*** **Unit 4 Assessment answers**

Unit 5

Rules to Know

1. When writing an address, capitalize the names of people, streets, cities, and states. Capitalize an abbreviation for any type of street or road and put a period after it. Put a comma between the city and the state. Capitalize both letters in the state abbreviation, but do not put a period after it.

   ➤ **Jenny Smith**

   300 Maple Street

   Madison, WI 56021

2. Be careful not to confuse these words: *are/our, you're/your.*

   are — a verb

   our — shows something that belongs to you and at least one other person

   you're — a contraction for "you are"

   your — a pronoun that shows ownership

   ➤ <u>**Are**</u> **you coming to** <u>**our**</u> **house today?**

   ➤ <u>**You're**</u> **the youngest member of** <u>**your**</u> **family.**

3. A past tense verb tells about something that has already happened. Add *ed* to most verbs to show past tense. If the word has a single vowel and ends with a consonant, double the last consonant before adding *ed*. If the word ends with an *e*, drop the final *e* before adding *ed*.

   ➤ **Yesterday, the boy** <u>**walked**</u> **home.**

   ➤ **The rabbit** <u>**hopped**</u> **away.**

   ➤ **My mom** <u>**baked**</u> **a cake for my birthday.**

4. The past tense of some verbs is made by changing the spelling.

   ➤ **Last week my dog** <u>**ran**</u> **away.**

   ➤ **We** <u>**bought**</u> **some milk at the store.**

   ➤ **He** <u>**drew**</u> **a picture in art class.**

5. A present tense verb shows something is happening now. Add *s* or *es* to most verbs if the subject is one person, place, thing, or animal. Do not add *s* or *es* to a verb if the subject is *I* or *you* or if the subject means more than one.

   ➤ **She** <u>**cooks**</u> **supper.**　　➤ **He** <u>**likes**</u> **to swim.**

   ➤ **They** <u>**cook**</u> **supper.**　　➤ **The boys** <u>**like**</u> **to swim.**

   ➤ **I** <u>**cook**</u> **supper.**　　➤ **You** <u>**like**</u> **to swim.**

your my best friend said ryan

we walk on davids beach last summer

to winter month are december and january

the jolly snowman is my favorite book

can you come two are
house on saturday

that boys cat runned
away last sunday

me and my brother
likes to read

new years day was on
january 1 2005

her didnt sea my
knew dog

mrs baker said im
gonna makes cookies

him goed too karens
house yesterday at 300

andy cook
18 robin drive
albany ny 07682

january 13 2004

dear aunt sue

thank you four the

great christmas present

your niece

molly

is pats pizza on hill
drive asked max

---

its snowing shouted
brads little sister

did amy makes all the
dress for the dance

are band play in a
show last friday knight

we aint gonna ride in him car said rick

susan davis

203 main street

san diego ca 97361

january 20 2004

dear tom

im having fun on my

vacation

your friend

glen

Unit 5 — Assessment

Name: _____ Date: _____

1. mrs baker said im gonna makes cookies

2. andy cook
18 robin drive
albany ny 07682

3. we walk on davids beach last summer

Score all words, group of numbers, or punctuation marks in these sentences as one point each, whether or not a correction is needed.

Score: _____ /32 _____ %

Unit 5 — Assessment

Answer Key

    M   B   I

1. mrs. baker said, "i'm going to gonna makes cookies."

    A   C

2. andy cook

      R   D

    18 robin drive

    A   NY

    albany, ny 07682

    W walked D

3. we walk on david's

    beach last summer.

Unit 5

Answer Key

1. "You're my best friend," said Ryan.

2. We walked on David's beach last summer.***

3. Two winter months are December and January.

4. <u>The Jolly Snowman</u> is my favorite book.

5. Can you come to our house on Saturday?

6. That boy's cat ran away last Sunday.

7. My brother and I like to read.

8. New Year's Day was on January 1, 2005.

9. She didn't see my new dog.

10. Mrs. Baker said, "I'm going to make cookies."***

11. He went to Karen's house yesterday at 3:00.

12. Andy Cook***
    18 Robin Drive
    Albany, NY 07682

13.   January 13, 2004
    Dear Aunt Sue,
        Thank you for the great Christmas present!
            Your niece,
            Molly

14. "Is Pat's Pizza on Hill Drive?" asked Max.

15. "It's snowing!" shouted Brad's little sister.

16. Did Amy make all the dresses for the dance?

17. Our band played in a show last Friday night.

18. "We aren't going to ride in his car," said Rick.

19. Susan Davis
    203 Main Street
    San Diego, CA 97361

20.   January 20, 2004
    Dear Tom,
        I'm having fun on my vacation!
            Your friend,
            Glen

***Unit 5 Assessment answers

Unit 6
Rules to Know

1. Some nouns change their spelling instead of adding *s* or *es* to mean "more than one." A few nouns can mean either one or more than one with the same spelling. Here are a few examples of these irregular plural nouns:

man → men   **sheep → sheep**   **tooth → teeth**

child → children   **woman → women**   **deer → deer**

foot → feet   **mouse → mice**

2. The verbs *am*, *are*, *is*, *was*, and *were* are not action words, instead they tell what someone or something is like.

Use *am* with the word *I*. Use *is* and *are* when talking about what is happening now. Use *was* and *were* when talking about things that have already happened.

Use *is* and *was* when talking about one person, place, thing, or animal. Use *are* and *were* when talking about more than one person, place, thing, or animal and with the word *you*.

➢ **I <u>am</u> six years old.**   →   **You <u>are</u> six years old.**
➢ **Jim <u>is</u> seven years old.**   →   **Last year Jim <u>was</u> six.**
➢ **Kate and Nate <u>are</u> eight.**   →   **They <u>were</u> seven last year.**

3. A negative is a word like *no*, *not*, *none*, or *never*. A contraction with the word *not* is also a negative. Do not use two negatives together in a sentence.

➢ **He <u>doesn't</u> have <u>no</u> money. →**   **He <u>doesn't</u> have <u>any</u> money.**
➢ **She <u>never</u> had <u>no</u> lunch.**   →   **She <u>never</u> had <u>any</u> lunch.**
➢ **<u>Can't</u> you see <u>nothing</u>?**   →   **<u>Can't</u> you see <u>anything</u>?**

4. The subject of a sentence tells who the sentence is about. A noun or a pronoun can be the subject of a sentence. Do not use both a noun and pronoun to mean the same person or thing in a sentence.

➢ **<u>The girl she</u> went skating. →**   **<u>The girl</u> went skating.**
➢ **<u>Tom he</u> came to my house. →**   **<u>Tom</u> came to my house.**
➢ **<u>Jill and I we</u> like to play.**   →   **<u>Jill and I</u> like to play.**

is groundhogs day on tuesday asked kay

did punxsutawney phil sea him shadow

valentines day will bee
on february 14 2005

the to mans saw for
deers in the woulds

ray he buyed the book
jack and the beanstalk

petes dog doesnt do no
tricks

eric said mr north work
at first state bank

the girl's they was
jumping rope last knight

is valentines day in
january or february

happy valentines day
shouted miss carson

february 11 2005

dear uncle mark

thanks for the birthday

gift its very nice

your nephew

mike

ryan green
97 oak boulevard
denver co 82743

we dont have no art
class today at 900

i is gonna lose to
tooths soon

on valentines day me
got hearts flowers and
candy

dont never play with
matches said mr bell

seth said im gonna go
two nicoles house on
friday

february 18 2005

dear dr rizzo

thank you for letting are class visit you're office.

you're friend

pat

ryan bill and jack is
my friend

me and anna water
the bushs yesterday

Unit 6 — Assessment

Name: _____ Date: _____

1. <u>petes dog doesnt do</u> <u>no tricks</u>

2. <u>the girl's they was</u> <u>jumping rope last</u> <u>knight</u>

3. <u>ryan bill and jack</u> <u>is my friend</u>

Score all words, group of numbers, or punctuation marks in these sentences as one point each, whether or not a correction is needed.

Score: _____ /28 _____ %

Unit 6 — Assessment

Answer Key

P
1. ~~pete's~~ dog doesn't do any
~~no~~ tricks.

T   girls   were
2. ~~the~~ ~~girl's~~ ~~they~~ ~~was~~

jumping rope last

~~k~~night.

R   b   J
3. ~~ryan,~~ ~~bill,~~ and ~~jack~~ are
~~is~~ my friend~~s~~.

Unit 6
Answer Key

1. "Is Groudhog's Day on Tuesday?" asked Kay.

2. Did Punxsutawney Phil see his shadow?

3. Valentine's Day will be on February 14, 2005.

4. The two men saw four deer in the woods.

5. Ray bought the book <u>Jack and the Beanstalk</u>.

6. Pete's dog doesn't do any tricks.***

7. Eric said, "Mr. North works at First State Bank."

8. The girls were jumping rope last night.***

9. Is Valentine's Day in January or February?

10. "Happy Valentine's Day!" shouted Miss Carson.

11.   February 11, 2005

Dear Uncle Mark,

Thanks for the birthday gift. It's very nice.

          Your nephew,

          Mike

12. Ryan Green

97 Oak Boulevard

Denver, CO 82743

13. We don't have any art class today at 9:00.

14. I am going to lose two teeth soon.

15. On Valentine's Day I got hearts, flowers, and candy.

16. "Don't ever play with matches!" said Mr. Bell.

17. Seth said, "I'm going to go to Nicole's house on Friday."

18.   February 18, 2005

Dear Dr. Rizzo,

    Thank you for letting our class visit your office.

          Your friend,

          Pat

19. Ryan, Bill, and Jack are my friends.***

20. Anna and I watered the bushes yesterday.

***Unit 6 Assessment answers*

doesnt dr seuss have a
birthday in march

their is some gooses
said the to girl's

march 2 2005

dear jenny

can you come two my

party on sunday at 130

your friend

meg

the first day of spring
is march 20 2005

me and ken ain't
gonna get a knew car

well read the three pigs today said jan

monday were to windy two fly a kite

jared and meg has a
dog named shelby

the leprechauns said
happy st patricks day

bill asked dont us
have no recess today

matt olson
2320 cherry ave
dayton oh 46297

doris said i like two

read cook and play golf

will easter come in

march or april this year

both first grade class

goed too the library

the to cat was chasing

the too mouses

them is coming two are house at 600 on friday

the five boy plays ball yesterday

my mom she is mrs betty king

alissa swimmed fast and one the race

march 20 2005

dear mr carter

your a great coach i

had fun in soccer

sincerely

paul

Unit 7 — Assessment

Name: _____ Date: _____

1. the leprechauns said happy st patricks day

2. them is coming two are house at 600 on friday

3. my mom she is mrs betty king

Score all words, group of numbers, or punctuation marks in these sentences as one point each, whether or not a correction is needed.

Score: _____ /34 _____%

Unit 7 — Assessment

Answer Key

1. T
~~the~~ ~~leprechauns~~ ~~said,~~
   H   S   P   D (! or .)
   ~~"happy st. patrick's day."~~

They are   to
2. ~~them is coming two~~

   our
   ~~are house at 6:00 on~~
   F
   ~~friday.~~
   M   M
3. ~~my mom she is mrs.~~
   B   K
   ~~betty king.~~

Unit 7

Answer Key

1. Doesn't Dr. Seuss have a birthday in March?

2. "There are some geese," said the two girls.

3.   March 2, 2005
   Dear Jenny,
      Can you come to my party on Sunday at 1:30?
         Your friend,
         Meg

4. The first day of spring is March 20, 2005.

5. Ken and I aren't going to get a new car.

6. "We'll read <u>The Three Pigs</u> today," said Jan.

7. Monday was too windy to fly a kite.

8. Jared and Meg have a dog named Shelby.

9. The leprechauns said, "Happy St. Patrick's Day!"***

10. Bill asked, "Don't we have any recess today?"

11. Matt Olson
    2320 Cherry Ave.
    Dayton, OH 46297

12. Doris said, "I like to read, cook, and play golf."

13. Will Easter come in March or April this year?

14. Both first grade classes went to the library.

15. The two cats were chasing the two mice.

16. They are coming to our house at 6:00 on Friday.***

17. The five boys played ball yesterday.

18. My mom is Mrs. Betty King.***

19. Alissa swam fast and won the race!

20.   March 20, 2005
    Dear Mr. Carter,
       You're a great coach! I had fun in soccer.
          Sincerely,
          Paul

***Unit 7 Assessment answers**

kim said today we red the book peter rabbit

aunt jan live in vermont said dan

doesnt mrs jones teach
at highview school

did you no that earth
day is april 22 2005

for easter me want candy eggs and toys

we never do nothing fun yelled ben

uncle jim he flyed to
honolulu hawaii

all the flower and bush
are starting two grow

dad watch jim play soccer last sunday

ain't the play gonna start at 400 he asked

april 11 2005

dear grandpa

it was good two sea you

after you're trip

best wishes

jeff

deb strong

15 south shore dr

green hill ar 60391

chuck and alan they

is having fun

me and tim is going
two are grandmas house

him doesnt get no
allowance this week

they ain't gonna go said mikes brother

that boys hat is to big said the girl

april 18 2005

dear mom and dad

camp is fun ill sea you

soon

with love

robbie

beths too cat's was named muff and puff

did you no that april showers bring may flowers

Unit 8 — Assessment

Name: _____ Date: _____

1. <u>for easter me want candy eggs and toys</u>

2. <u>dad watch jim play soccer last sunday</u>

3. <u>deb strong</u>
<u>15 south shore dr</u>
<u>green hill ar 60391</u>

Score all words, group of numbers, or punctuation marks in these sentences as one point each, whether or not a correction is needed.

Score: _____/33 _____%

Unit 8 — Assessment

Answer Key

      F   E   I

1. for easter me want candy,

   eggs, and toys.
   D   Jim

2. dad watched jim play
                   S

   soccer last sunday.
  D S

3. deb strong
        S   S   D

   15 south shore dr.
   G   H   AR

   green hill, ar 60391

Unit 8

Answer Key

1. Kim said, "Today we read the book <u>Peter Rabbit</u>."

2. "Aunt Jan lives in Vermont," said Dan.

3. Doesn't Mrs. Jones teach at Highview School?

4. Did you know that Earth Day is April 22, 2005?

5. For Easter I want candy, eggs, and toys.***

6. "We never do anything fun!" yelled Ben.

7. Uncle Jim flew to Honolulu, Hawaii.

8. All the flowers and bushes are starting to grow.

9. Dad watched Jim play soccer last Sunday.***

10. "Isn't the play going to start at 4:00?" he asked.

11.   April 11, 2005
    Dear Grandpa,
        It was good to see you after your trip.
            Best wishes,
            Jeff

12. Deb Strong***
    15 South Shore Dr.
    Green Hill, AR 60391

13. Chuck and Alan are having fun.

14. Tim and I are going to our grandma's house.

15. He doesn't get any allowance this week.

16. "They aren't going to go," said Mike's brother.

17. "That boy's hat is too big," said the girl.

18.   April 18, 2005
    Dear Mom and Dad,
        Camp is fun! I'll see you soon.
            With love,
            Robbie

19. Beth's two cats were named Muff and Puff.

20. Did you know that April showers bring May flowers?

***Unit 8 Assessment answers

did her gets a may
basket on may day

did you plant too
tree's on arbor day

cindy asked do you wanna played with me

were over hear brian shouted loudly

were gonna go sea a
knew movie at 600

are country is the united
states of america

me and my cousin we
rided him bike yesterday

did mrs harris read the
gingerbread man too us

i blowed out the candles

and made to wish

do you like two right

stories songs or poems

may 11 2005

dear mrs berg

thank you for taking

us on a field trip

your student

alan

roxy kennedy

641 northside ave

sioux falls sd 71237

kyles friend doesnt

live buy him no more

is you're knew pool six foots deep asked fred

do you no that memorial day is in may

all the lunchs is made

four are picnic today

too dog's is to many

two walk by yourself

may 18 2005

dear sally

i cant wait too sea you

in june

your pal

julie

is memorial day always
on a monday or tuesday

have a great summer
class said there teacher

Unit 9 — Assessment

Name: _____ Date: _____

1. are country is the united states of america

2. did mrs harris read the gingerbread man too us

3.   may 18 2005

dear sally

    i cant wait too

sea you in june

       your pal

       julie

Score all words, group of numbers, or punctuation marks in these sentences as one point each, whether or not a correction is needed.

Score: _____ /42 _____%

Unit 9 — Assessment

Answer Key

Our   U   S

1. ~~are~~ country is the ~~united states~~

    A

~~of america.~~

  D   M   H   T

2. ~~did mrs. harris read the~~

  G   M

~~gingerbread man to us?~~

  M

3. ~~may 18, 2005~~

  D S

~~dear sally,~~

  I   to see   J (! or .)

~~i can't wait too sea you in june!~~

  Y

~~your pal,~~

  J

~~julie~~

Unit 9

Answer Key

1. Did she get a May basket on May Day?

2. Did you plant two trees on Arbor Day?

3. Cindy asked, "Do you want to play with me?"

4. "We're over here!" Brian shouted loudly.

5. We're going to go see a new movie at 6:00.

6. Our country is the United States of America.***

7. My cousin and I rode his bike yesterday.

8. Did Mrs. Harris read <u>The Gingerbread Man</u> to us?***

9. I blew out the candles and made two wishes.

10. Do you like to write stories, songs, or poems?

11. May 11, 2005
   Dear Mrs. Berg,
      Thank you for taking us on a field trip.
         Your student,
         Alan

12. Roxy Kennedy
   641 Northside Ave.
   Sioux Falls, SD 71237

13. Kyle's friend doesn't live by him any more.

14. "Is your new pool six feet deep?" asked Fred.

15. Do you know that Memorial Day is in May?

16. All the lunches are made for our picnic today.

17. Two dogs are too many to walk by yourself.

18. May 18, 2005***
   Dear Sally,
     I can't wait to see you in June!
         Your pal,
         Julie

19. Is Memorial Day always on a Monday or Tuesday?

20. "Have a great summer class!" said their teacher.

***Unit 9 Assessment answers

Cumulative Assessment

Name: _____   Date: _____   Score: _____/160

1. we walk on davids beach last summer
   (From page 81, #2)

2. ryan bill and jack is my friend
   (From page 96, #19)

3. those box were to heavy for max too lift
   (From page 51, #9)

4. today ain't december 9 2004
   (From page 66, #2)

5. petes dog doesnt do no tricks
   (From page 96, #6)

Cumulative Assessment *(cont.)*

6. andy cook
18 robin drive
albany ny 07682
(From page 81, #12)

7. them is coming two are
house at 600 on friday
(From page 110, #16)

8. me and my cousin we rided
him bike yesterday
(From page 138, #7)

9. is jills favorite book the
three pigs
(From page 51, #10)

10. santa said its very cold at
the north pole
(From page 66, #9)

Cumulative Assessment *(cont.)*

11. we never do nothing fun yelled ben

(From page 124, #6)

12. is valentines day in january or february

(From page 96, #9)

13. the to cat was chasing the too mouses

(From page 110, #5)

14.
                                      april 11 2005
    dear grandpa
        it was good two sea you
    after you're trip
                              best wishes
                                    jeff

(From page 124, #11)

15. are them going on a trip two canada

(From page 35, #17)

Name _____

My
Daily Editing
Skills Practice

Rules to
Know

Writing Form

Sentences

Name: _____ Date: _____

_____
- -
_____
_____
- -
_____
_____
- -
_____
_____
- -
_____

Name: _____ Date: _____

_____
- -
_____
_____
- -
_____
_____
- -
_____
_____
- -
_____

Writing Form

Friendly Letter

Name: _____ Date: _____

_____

_____

_____

_____

_____

_____

_____

_____

_____

_____

_____

_____

_____

_____

_____

_____

_____

_____